The Mary Rose
in a Nutshell

The Mary Rose in a Nutshell

M
MadeGlobal Publishing

For more information on
MadeGlobal Publishing, visit our website:
www.madeglobal.com

Cover: Artist impression of the Mary Rose
by Mihaly Kovesdi

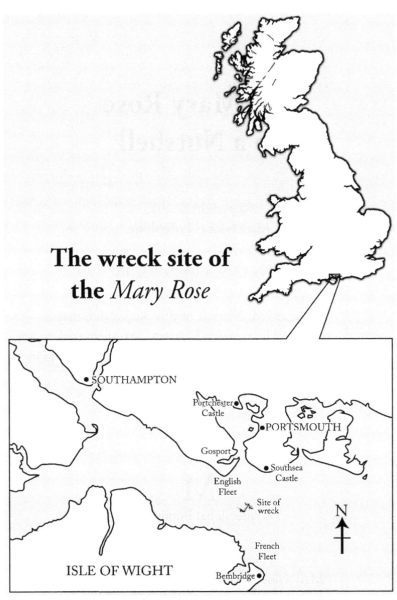

The wreck site of
the *Mary Rose*

SOUTHAMPTON

Portchester
Castle

●PORTSMOUTH

Gosport

Southsea
Castle

English
Fleet

Site of
wreck

N

French
Fleet

ISLE OF WIGHT

Bembridge ●

History
"In a Nutshell"
Series

Contents

Figure 1 - Detail showing what may be the *Mary Rose*.
The Embarkation of Henry VIII at Dover 1520.
Photo copyright © 2016 Philip Roberts

INTRODUCTION

It is very easy to look at the *Mary Rose* and see nothing more than just a very old ship. But the *Mary Rose* was a high-tech, state of the art warship built by King Henry VIII at the beginning of his reign. He was very fond of the *Mary Rose* and made her his flagship in many battles and skirmishes. However, during an engagement with a French invasion fleet she disastrously sank. Henry was 'oppressed with sorowe'.[1]

Dan Snow wonderfully summarises the event by saying in his video presentation for the Mary Rose Museum: "On that fateful day in 1545, life stopped abruptly for the 500 men on board. Their belongings, the tools they used, their clothes, the food they ate, the plates and bowls they ate from, their bones – everything was found just as it had been when the ship sank. This ancient maritime disaster has provided a huge collection of real objects that were being used by real people – one moment in time, preserved forever."

---

1.   Richard Hooker, the contemporary biographer of Sir Peter Carew, after
      1575 wrote *The Lyffe of Sir Peter Carew*. Published by Phillips (1839, 96-151).
      Extract is from pp. 109-11.

Figure 2 - In 1520 the Mary Rose was called to duty at the meeting between Henry VIII and Francis I at the Field of the Cloth of Gold. The Mary Rose is believed to be the ship on the far right of the painting.

The Embarkation of Henry VIII at Dover 1520

Photo copyright © 2016 Philip Roberts

THE ORIGINS OF THE MARY ROSE

When Henry Tudor came to the throne in 1485, his kingship ended a long period of civil war in England called the War of the Roses. However, his claim to the throne was very unstable. After his early years in power, Henry VII successfully warded off any competition for the crown and then he sued for peace. To achieve this he married his eldest daughter Margaret to James IV, King of Scotland (a long-time enemy), and his only surviving son Henry to Katherine of Aragon, the daughter to a very powerful ally, the King of Spain.

When Henry Tudor died, his remaining son became Henry VIII on Saturday 21 April 1509. As a young man he was a keen student and through studying history books came to admire King Henry V's strength and mightiness in reclaiming lost territory in France, particularly his famous victory at Agincourt in 1415, despite being greatly outnumbered. Unlike his father, who pursued peace, Henry VIII had a taste for war.

As with his namesake Henry V, the French were also to become Henry VIII's enemy. The Venetian ambassador, Andrea

Badoer, commented on 25 April 1509, just three days after Henry had become king, that, "the king is magnificent, liberal and a great enemy of the French,"[2] and then on the next day, another Venetian courtier simply stated in a letter that, "the king swore, *de more*, immediately after his coronation to make war on the King of France. Soon we shall hear that he has invaded France."[3]

In 1511, Henry VIII joined the Holy League, a combination of King Ferdinand of Spain, Pope Julius II, and the republic of Venice, to act in union against France. Henry planned to conquer Bordeaux, while King Ferdinand, the pope and the republic of Venice intended to attack other French regions. Henry led an army into France in 1513 and captured Tournai, while the Scots, an ally of France, invaded Northern England in retaliation.

Henry wanted to make his mark at home and abroad. He had a personal desire for success in battle. One of the ways Henry achieved this was to create the country's first permanent warships. He did this by building, manning, maintaining and arming the ships at his own expense. Today we call it the Royal Navy, Henry called it his 'Army by Sea'.[4] Previously, when war had to be fought at sea, merchant ships were commandeered and adapted for battle by building fighting platforms for men armed with longbows. All of this was about to change. Henry inherited five ships from his father Henry VII, but to add to his fleet as soon as he came to the throne, Henry commissioned the building of two new ships, the *Peter Pomegranate* and her sister ship, the *Mary Rose*. On 9 June 1511, Robert Brigandine wrote a letter to do with payments for the construction of ships. This was the first mention of the *Mary Rose* by name.[5] The renowned shipbuilding town of Portsmouth was chosen to construct his new ships.

---

2.   Letters and Papers, Foreign and Domestic, of the reign of Henry VIII
3.   Ibid, 19
4.   6 May 1512 Letter from Henry VIII to Cardinal Bainbridge
5.   Holograph letter dated Woolwich, 9 June 1511, Brigandyn to Mr Pashid (CSP I-I, 1393, p. 640; Knighton and Loades 2002, text2)

THE NAME "MARY ROSE"

Early thoughts were that the *Mary Rose* was named after the king's sister Mary, who was married to Charles Brandon, 1ˢᵗ Duke of Suffolk. However, after considering sources available, it is more likely that she was named after the Virgin Mary, as it was a custom in medieval times to give fighting ships scriptural names. For instance, Henry V's great ships included *Holigost, Jesus of Lubeck, Henri Grace à Dieu* (the largest of them all) and *Trinity Royal*, his flagship at the time of the Battle of Agincourt. Also, in 1464 *John Evangelist* and in 1470 *St Peter* were ships belonging to King Edward IV.

Henry VII, however, did introduce two vessels with royal names, *Sovereign* and *Regent*. King Henry VIII's demonstration of the link between church and state was to be in the ship *Henri Grace à Dieu*. This name indicates the king's view that he ruled 'by the Grace of God' and received his kingly powers from God. His fleet would be the means to show his divine authority. In 1512, Henry purchased the *Mary Lovet* and renamed her *Gabriel Royal*, and he acquired the *John Baptist* and the *Christ* in the same year. *Trinity Royal* was built in 1519 and Henry purchased *Jesus of Lubeck* in 1544.

The name of the *Mary Rose*'s sister ship *Peter Pomegranate* combined the symbol of Katherine of Aragon (the pomegranate) with Peter. Who is this Peter? There was no one in the Houses of Tudor or Aragon with the name Peter. It could only refer to a scriptural character, the Apostle Peter. In the year of the *Mary Rose*'s first voyage in 1511, Henry went to the shrine of Our Lady of Walsingham to pay homage after the birth of their son, who sadly died at 52 days old. At this point in his life, the king still had great respect and love for the reverence of the Virgin Mary. Also, naming a ship after his sister and not his wife, who he was very much in love with, would have been a strange decision.[6] Indeed, Katherine did eventually get a ship named after her, the *Katherine Pleasance*, but not until 1518. Whichever Mary she was named after, there is no doubt that the rose refers to the Tudor rose.

6.   Letters and Papers, Foreign and Domestic, of the reign of Henry VIII Vol I, Pt I, 119

FITTING OUT THE MARY ROSE

The *Mary Rose* and the *Peter Pomegranate* were towed from Portsmouth to the Thames at London in September 1511, where coats of white and green, for the master, the quartermasters, the boatswain, and twenty-four soldiers, were purchased. These coats were presumably a type of uniform. Further money was paid a little later for more coats of the same, for the master and thirty-four of his company, both mariners and sailors. As the costs were shared between the *Mary Rose* and the *Peter Pomegranate*, it is uncertain how many men served in each ship.[7]

The next destination for the two ships was probably the Tower of London, from which the guns could be installed. They were also rigged and decking was constructed. From September 1511 to April 1512, more fitting-out took place. In April, John Browne, described as the king's painter and ship decorator, applied the streamers to fly from the masts. An inventory in 1514 shows that

---

7.   (CSP I-II, 3608, p. 1497; Knighton and Loades 2002, text 4)

there were three streamers, flags and banners. Thomas Sperte was then the master and David Boner was the purser of the *Mary Rose.*

The fitting-out ended in April 1512 with a payment of £77 0s.3d. to Cornelius Johnson for making guns, gunstocks, bands, chambers, etc., and a payment of £38 6s.2d. for delivering gunpowder chambers to the *Mary Rose* and *Peter Pomegranate.*[8]

Figure 3 - A wrought iron breech loading cannon from the wreck of the *Mary Rose.* Photo copyright © 2016 Philip Roberts

8.   (CSP I-II, 3608, p.1498)

HOW WELL DID THE
MARY ROSE SAIL?

There is a record of how well the *Mary Rose* sailed. In March 1513 the admiral, Sir Edward Howard, brought the fleet, including his flagship the *Mary Rose*, to the north-east coast of Kent, where he ordered a race to test the ships abilities. They did not start in a line but instead some were as much as 4 miles ahead of the *Mary Rose*. Nevertheless, the order of arrival revealed which were the fastest ships: *Mary Rose, Sovereign, Nicholas, Leonard of Dartmouth, Mary George, Henry of Southampton, Anne, Nicholas Montrygo, Katherine Pleasance* and *Mary James*. Howard stressed his delight in the *Mary Rose* by saying, "…sche is the noblest shipp of sayle (of any) gret ship, at this howr, that I trow (know) in Cristendom." [9]

---

9.   Sir Edward Howard to Henry VIII, 22 March 1513. Brit. Lib: Cotton MS. Caligula D. VI, f. 103

OFFICERS AND CREW

We are blessed to have records of the crew of the *Mary Rose*, showing that she was a vital ship. Many documents list the officers and the number of crew. One of these documents is held by Ian Friel, exhibition notes in the Mary Rose Trust archive. Here are the names of those we know:

OFFICERS

- Sep 1511 Master: John Clerke
- Oct – Nov 1511 Master: Thomas Sperte; Purser: David Boner
- Nov 1511 – Jan 1512 Master: Thomas Sperte; Purser: John Lawden
- Feb 1512 Purser: John Lawden
- Apr – Jul 1512 Chief Captain and Admiral of the Fleet: Sir Edward Howard
- Oct 1512 Admiral: Sir Edward Howard; ?status: Sir John Wyndeham; Master: Thomas Sperte

- 1513 Captain: Sir Edward Howard; Master: Thomas Sperte
- May – Aug 1513 Admiral: Lord Thomas Howard; Captain: Edward Braye
- Jul 1513 Surgeon: Rob Symson
- 1513 Purser: John Brerely; Gunner: Andrew Fysche; Master: Thomas Pert
- Jan – Feb 1514 Captain: Edward Braye
- 1514 Captain: Sir Henry Shernburne
- Mar 1514 Master: John Browne
- Apr 1514 Captain: Sir Henry Sherburne
- Oct 1517 Keeper: Wm. Mewe, plus 4 men
- Jun 1522 Lord High Admiral: Thomas Howard; Master: John Browne
- 1524 Ship Keeper: Fadere Conner

SOLDIERS, MARINERS, GUNNERS AND OTHERS

The numbers of men on board during active service are listed as below:

Date	Soldiers	Mariners	Gunners	Others	Total
1512 summer	411	206	120	22	729
1512 October	?	120	20	20	160
1513 Early	?	200	?	?	200
1513 Late	?	102	6	?	108
c. 1522	126	244	30	2	400
1524	185	200	20	?	405
1545	185	200	30	?	415

THE ANTHONY ANTHONY ROLL

The Anthony Anthony Roll was presented to Henry VIII in 1546, a year after she sank, when it was thought that the *Mary Rose* could still be salvaged. It is a declaration of King Henry's fifty-eight ships composed by Anthony Anthony, clerk of the ordnance at the Tower of London. The book is the only Tudor illustration we have of the *Mary Rose*.

Unfortunately, there is little information about the form and construction of the ship. Nowhere is there written evidence to say that the ship is a carrack or that the ship's structure was built by overlapped planks or by connecting planks secured with pitch to waterproof the ship. This is only established by the picture in the Anthony Anthony Roll. What it is depicting is not necessarily the most artistically accurate illustration of a naval ship, but what it does show is a four-masted sailing vessel bristling with guns. It also shows a main deck with another two rows of guns on top of it.

It is absolutely incredible to look at this illustration and to admire the hand that put this fantastic source of information together. The artist must have been somebody who had a detailed

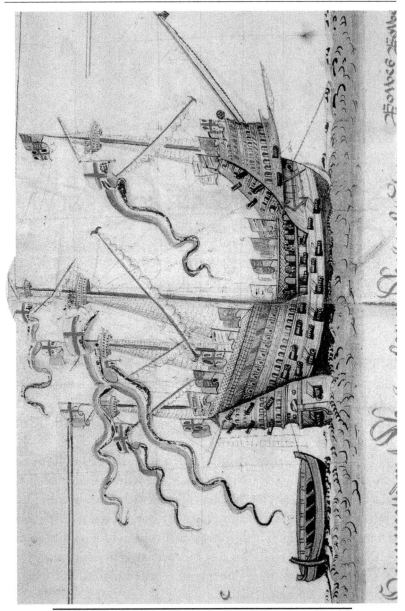

Figure 4 - The *Mary Rose* from the Anthony Anthony Roll circa 1546. Photo by Gerry Bye.

knowledge of the ship. He must have once been on board her and was passionate enough to put together what is undeniably a beautiful illustration, giving us the only illustrated inventory from the sixteenth century. It states that there were 200 mariners, 185 soldiers and 30 gunners on board the *Mary Rose* in 1545.

The *Mary Rose* is shown in the Anthony Anthony Roll as having four masts and a bowsprit: a foremast, a main mast, a main mizzen mast and a bonaventure mizzen mast. A clue exists in the *Calendar of State Papers of Henry VIII* regarding the height of the mast of the *Mary Rose*, for on 21 March 1538, G Lovedaye wrote to Wriothesley: "There is making for the Admiral a ship of the same fashion as the Peterpomegarnet, but greater. Her mast is 150 feet long." This means that the *Peter Pomegranate*'s hull was only two-thirds the size of the *Mary Rose*, again proving that she was a formidable warship.

THE KING'S FAVOURITE SHIP

King Henry VIII was very fond of the *Mary Rose* and made her his flagship for many skirmishes. This gives her a unique position in naval history to be the first flagship of the country's new Royal Navy. For the *Mary Rose*'s first battle against the French, Sir Edward Howard was commissioned to be the admiral, an old jousting companion of the king.[10] Naval warfare in Tudor England was seen as the pursuit of personal glory, much like jousting. Unfortunately for Howard, he was killed two years later leading an attack on the French coast, but not from the *Mary Rose*.

During her time in the king's service, she served in wars against France. The first was the Battle of Brest in 1512, when the English defeated the French fleet decisively.[11]

She was almost involved in a war with Scotland, but the English land army had already won the day at Flodden on 9 September 1513. Then, in 1514, a treaty of perpetual peace between England and France was arranged between Cardinal Thomas Wolsey and

10.   (CSP, I-II, 1132, p.540)
11.   (CSP Venetian, II, 1509-1519, 199, pp.80-1)

French ambassadors, which left the *Mary Rose* laid-up in Deptford on the River Thames for six years.[12]

She came back in service in 1520 to escort Henry VIII and his very large court across the Channel to meet the French king. This meeting became known as the Field of Cloth of Gold.[13] The meeting was supposed to strengthen the fragile relationship between the two kings. It drastically failed. War broke out again and the *Mary Rose* was back at sea. She was involved in a successful attack on Morlaix in 1522. Cardinal Wolsey wrote to King Henry VIII: "Pleaseth it your grace to be advertised that at this time I have advertised the King's grace of the taking of Morlaix."[14] After that war ended in 1525, she was again laid-up, first in Portsmouth,[15] and then for ten years on the Thames.[16]

---

12.   (CSP I-II, 3137 pp. 1338-1340)
13.   (CSP III-I, 704, p. 239)
14.   (To Cardinal Wolsey, Morlaix Haven, Brittany, Tuesday 3 July, 1522. Public
       Record Office – SPI/25)
15.   (CSP IV-III, 6138, p. 2739)
16.   (CSP IV-I, 1714, p. 762)

REFITTED

Very little is known of the *Mary Rose* from late 1528 until 1539, due to the lack of documents. There is some confusion around published statements that the *Mary Rose* was believed to have been 'rebuilt' in 1536 and/or 1539/40. However, Thomas Cromwell did write in 1536 that the *Mary Rose* was "made new".[17]

Dendrochronology, or tree-ring dating, of timbers in the *Mary Rose* prove that alterations certainly did occur around 1535-6 and maybe she was refitted again a few years later. Timbers were added and deck heights altered to make the ship stronger, allowing her to carry much heavier guns. By 1545 she could carry thirty guns on carriages, whereas in 1514 she only had five. Also, gun-ports were cut into her sides making the *Mary Rose* one of the first ships to carry cannon below the top deck. She began as a troop transporter ship but now the *Mary Rose* was a formidable, high tech warship.

---

17.   (CSP X, 1231, p. 513)

With the riches from the monasteries, Henry became the wealthiest English monarch ever. He also spent a fortune on clover-leaf-shaped coastal defensive fortifications all around the eastern and southern coasts of England, including Southsea Castle in Portsmouth.

Figure 5 - Southsea Castle
Photo by Geni via Wikimedia Commons

THE BATTLE OF THE SOLENT

Why did the French attack England in 1545?

A string of events angered the Catholic King of France. In 1529, Henry VIII had broken away from the pope as his spiritual leader and in 1533 he made himself the supreme head of the Church of England. Also, in the 1530s, he disbanded the Catholic monasteries, keeping their wealth for himself. The *Mary Rose* was involved in a successful attack on Boulogne in 1544. This English victory was the last straw to provoke the French into amassing a fleet to invade England.

The *Mary Rose* was called to defend Henry's kingdom against an enormous French invasion fleet of 225 ships carrying 30,000 men, three times bigger than that of the Spanish Armada fleet forty-three years later.

On the evening of 18 July 1545, dining on board the flagship for this battle and the biggest ship of the king's fleet *Henry Grace à Dieu*, King Henry VIII proclaimed Sir George Carew his vice admiral to sail as captain on the *Mary Rose*. Sir George Carew had led troops in Henry's successful attack on Boulogne.[18] Sir Roger Grenville served as an officer on the *Mary Rose* during the late stages of her lifetime but there is no solid evidence that he was on the ship the day it sank.

Henry had assembled his land army in Portsmouth, encamped on Southsea Common, ready to fight with their longbows, hand-held guns and cannons. This was to be one of the last European battles in which the longbow was used as a weapon of war, being replaced by weapons with gunpowder.

On 19 July 1545, Henry VIII stood on the ramparts of Southsea Castle proudly watching his ships fighting the French in what was to become known as the Battle of the Solent. The English fleet was close to Portsmouth Harbour while the French were nearby, off St Helen's Road anchorage on the Isle of Wight.

That evening, four French galleys, which were propelled by oarsmen, had been sent in advance of the rest of its fleet, rowed towards the English ships, firing their forward-facing guns. Two kilometres out from Portsmouth Harbour, cannons blazing, the *Mary Rose* fired her guns mounted on one side of the ship straight towards them. In readiness to fire again from the guns mounted on the other side, she immediately began to turn. As she turned, King Henry looked in absolute horror as she heeled over too far. Water gushed in through her open lower gun-ports and flooded the decks.

A standard procedure when fighting at close quarters was to cover the deck area with a canopy of netting to make it difficult for the enemy to board the ship. Unfortunately for the men on the *Mary Rose*, it proved to be a death trap for those caught underneath the netting. They would have had no chance of escaping. She sank at an alarming rate into the misty depths of the Solent.

Many reports of the sinking were written years later or by people who were not there, so these are not reliable accounts.

---

18.   Richard Hooker, the contemporary biographer of Sir Peter Carew, after
       1575 wrote *The Lyffe of Sir Peter Carew*. Published by Phillips
       (1839, 96-151). Extract is from pp. 109-11.

There is only one reliable account recorded at the time, five days after the sinking, by Van der Delft, ambassador to Charles V:

> *Towards the evening the ship (the Mary Rose) foundered, all the 500 men on board being drowned save about 25 or 30 servants, sailors and the like. Was told by a Fleming amongst the survivors that when she heeled over with the wind the water entered by the lowest row of gun-ports which had been left open after firing.*[19]

Sadly, the vice-admiral, Sir George Carew, went down with his ship.[20] His name is the only one we know for sure who was on board the ship on that day.

Many theories were developed as to why she sank – was she top-heavy and imbalanced? As previously stated, we know that Henry ordered a refit or two to increase the number of large guns. Or was there a strong gust of wind at just the wrong moment as she made that turn? Perhaps an unruly crew or captain. It is more than likely that it was a combination of these factors.

The event was such a tragedy that it was recorded in a painting for Sir Anthony Browne. It hung in Cowdray House until 1793, when the house caught fire and the painting was destroyed. Fortunately for us, an engraving was made by James Basire, the tutor of the famous English poet, painter and printmaker, William Blake.

The Battle of the Solent was inconclusive. Neither the English or the French were victorious. A report said that, "the Frenchmen landed in the Isle of Wight, where their captain (The Chevalier d'Aux) was slain and then driven to their ships."[21]

---

19.   (CSP XX-I, 1263, p.627)
20.   (CSP XX-II, 494, p. 213)
21.   (CSP XX-II, 494, p. 213)

Figure 6 - The Cowdray Engraving showing the wreck of the *Mary Rose* in the centre, the English fleet to the right and the French fleet to the left. Henry VIII is on horseback in the centre..

EARLY ATTEMPTS AT SALVAGE

The loss of the *Mary Rose* was enormous, especially financially. In a letter written by Charles Brandon, the Duke of Suffolk, to Sir William Paget, he says:

> *My Lorde Admyrall, being this present Friday at dynner with me, that he had a good hope of the waying upright of the Mary Rose, this afternone or tomorrow.*[22]

Henry VIII paid Venetian experts to salvage her. They immediately started to try to upright her by pulling on her masts and positioned lifting cables. The removal of sails and rigging was achieved by 5 August 1545, but attempts to put her upright on 8 August failed, breaking the foremast and possibly the main mast.[23] The whereabouts of the wreck site was not recorded.

---

22.   (CSP XX-II, 61, p. 30)
23.   (CSP XX-II, 951, p.473; Knighton and Loades 2002, text 76)

King Henry VIII outlived the *Mary Rose* by only two years. The *Mary Rose* went into obscurity while the king was transformed into legend.

Moving on almost 300 years. In 1818, a barn in Kent caught fire. A neighbour, John Deane, came to the rescue of the tied-up horses, but was unable to help because of dense smoke. Deane used his initiative by putting on a helmet from an old suit of armour and pushed a tube from a fire pump inside it to provide fresh air. It worked well. From this experience, his brother Charles later adapted the helmet and patented the idea as a diving helmet, and they began to explore underwater wrecks.

On 10 June 1836, Henry Abbinett, diver, was asked to look at some snagging of fishing nets and he discovered the timbers of a shipwreck. Then on 16 June, the Deane brothers, along with William Edwards, were diving in the Solent to salvage the wreck of the *Royal George*, the largest ship in the world at the time of its launch in 1756, which had foundered at Spithead in 1782. They were asked to investigate. They discovered a gun. At this location it could only be the *Mary Rose*. She had been re-discovered!

They initially used spades to dig holes and then resorted to using explosives to penetrate the hard silts, fortunately causing little damage to the hull. Over the next four years they brought to the surface objects such as great guns of bronze and wrought-iron, longbows, shot, part of the main mast and a grapnel. Most were sold to museums or at auction, but they had to abandon the project in 1840 due to lack of money.

MODERN DISCOVERY
AND EARLY EXCAVATION

The man who found the *Mary Rose* again was Alexander McKee. He spent ten years of his leisure time on the search, when no one but he thought it could ever be successful. Alex took up diving when he was 38 years old. He thought this was an opportunity that would come only once in his generation. He knew that the most important wreck in north-west Europe was somewhere there in the Solent and he wanted to spend his time on that, and he felt that even if he had failed, he would not have wasted his time because it was a well-worthwhile objective. McKee's scrapbooks tell the story of his search for the *Mary Rose*. There was no money to fund anything at all.

He and his small group from the Southsea Branch of the British Sub-Aqua Club systematically scoured the seabed at Spithead, diving from the stern of a local fishing boat. It was years before the Mary Rose Expedition, as it was then called, was lent a boat of its own and began to attract some public support.

McKee just didn't search the seabed at random, he was a military historian and conducted a very thorough programme of research into the wreck. This led him to a collection of watercolours made by the Deane brothers before 1840 and a study of the Cowdray engraving, which revealed that the topography of the landscape was incredibly accurate.

The approximate position of the wreck was also marked on an admiralty chart that McKee found in the Royal Navy's Hydrographic Office in 1966. This discovery was crucial. He knew that the Deanes had found nothing of the *Mary Rose* standing above the seabed, and so he was looking for an 'invisible' wreck under the seabed, 120 years later. The first thing he discovered was the wonderful, thick, black, gooey, mud and grey clay. It was very soft and he knew that the *Mary Rose* would have sunk into it very fast and that a lot of the ship would be down there, as this wonderful preservative would have kept the material in very good condition.

Nineteen sixty-six was the first year that sonar gear had been used for archaeological purposes. They were looking for an anomaly and found a 'W' feature, which was thought to be some of the decks of the *Mary Rose*. But to prove it they had to dig down. They dug between 6 and 9 feet using their hands.

Shortly after the discovery of the *Mary Rose*, archaeologist Margaret Rule was asked to join the team as a consultant. She had been the leading archaeologist at the excavation of the Roman palace at Fishbourne, near Chichester. The Mary Rose 1967 Committee was immediately formed. In 1968, a lease to an area of the seabed was granted from the Crown Estates Commissioners, providing legal protection for the site. The Mary Rose Committee could now mark the position of the *Mary Rose*.

Margaret Rule, who was in her 40s, learnt how to dive to investigate the wreck site herself. She built up a whole team of maritime archaeologists to lead the divers in what was the beginning of the world's largest ever underwater archaeological project. The 12.5m-long catamaran, *Roger Grenville*, was used as the dive boat. Divers worked very hard in 1968, with acoustic equipment being used to help them, by penetrating the seabed to reveal buried objects. With the search area now developed, two years later a wrought-iron gun, similar to those recovered by John Deane, was found.

In 1971, following a stormy winter, diver Percy Ackland spotted and recognised four timbers that were sticking up from the seabed. They were some of the frames of the ship. Later these were identified as the frames of the port side of the *Mary Rose*. Morrie Young, a former shipwright, had invaluable practical experience. Where no one could see clearly through the murky water, Young was able to identify parts of the ship simply by feeling.

As archaeology graduates in the late 1970s who took part in the diving programme, Christopher Dobbs and Alex Hildred are still today with the Mary Rose Trust as head of interpretation and curator of Ordinance respectively. Alex Hildred said in a documentary:

> *I don't know what makes people passionate about the Mary Rose. I just know that almost every single one of the volunteer divers that worked on the project shared a love of the Mary Rose that you just can't understand, you can't tell anybody else what it's like, it's there within your being. I think it's the fact that you have been involved with something that was the most important thing in your life. We lived, we ate, we slept on the dive vessel. Everything was about raising the Mary Rose and her objects. I think that feeling started with the first dive.*

Talking about the thrill of seeing the three ship's timbers protruding from the silt, Alex Hildred continues:

> *It was inconceivable how big the ship was. There were only a few timbers at that stage sticking up from the seabed. Because you couldn't see very far, you could not actually realise how big the ship was.*

Self-funded and reliant on donations and sponsorship, work continued on the timbers to reveal a ship-shape. In 1978 a trench was cut across the bow, revealing two decks in situ.

At the end of 1978, the committee had to confront several big decisions. *Should* the *Mary Rose* be completely excavated and raised? And secondly, *could* the hull be raised and safely? Two milestone meetings were held to answer these questions. They were attended by archaeologists, ship historians, naval architects, salvage consultants and structural engineers. Happily, the outcome was to excavate the hull with the view to raising it.

THE MARY ROSE TRUST

On 19 January 1979, the Mary Rose Trust was formed with His Royal Highness, Prince Charles agreeing to be president. A renowned board of trustees and an executive committee were formed. Margaret Rule was appointed archaeological director with overall responsibility for the excavation.

Now the Mary Rose Trust could in earnest start to raise the funds needed to carry on with their objectives. Prince Charles first dived on the site in 1975. His ninth dive was undertaken in 1982, just before the raising. He was also one of the first people to get close to the hull after she was raised and has maintained close ties with the project throughout. He spoke of diving conditions as "like diving in cold lentil soup" and of the experience he said: "For me it was a great thrill. A feeling of connection with Henry VIII made it even more intriguing."

Figure 7 - Prince Charles watching the raising of the *Mary Rose*

Figure 8 - The wreck surfaces

MAJOR EXCAVATION WORK

The operation now was on a massive scale. At the beginning of 1979, with the help of Portsmouth City Council, the newly formed Mary Rose Trust purchased a large salvage and diving vessel called the *Sleipner* from the Neptune Salvage Company in Gothenburg, to be the dive headquarters. She had previously been used as the 'mothership' during the recovery of the Swedish warship Vasa salvaged in 1961. She was anchored over the site from spring to late autumn. *Sleipner* accommodated a team of divers and diving archaeologists. A plan was made where the site could be covered over to preserve it if funds were not available to continue. However, work continued. The first thing to do was remove the upper level deposits from modern times to Tudor, and then the smelly silts above the Tudor levels with the objective of recovering all objects inside and immediately around the hull, strengthening the hull and then recovering the ship. Much work had to be carried out by hand or with the careful use of paintbrushes. Huge care had to be taken to ensure that no damage was caused. Decks, cabins, cannons, longbows, chests and tools were all exposed. All these items, one by one, were cautiously brought to the surface.

Diving is dangerous, no matter how carefully and strictly you organise it. Fifty feet below the surface, there is absolutely nothing you can do to protect yourself against a sudden, incapacitating medical event. A minor heart attack, a brief blackout or the beginnings of a fit would kill you, and even something much less serious could cause death. On 2 July 1980, the *Mary Rose* claimed a life. The day was calm and sunny and diving conditions were superb. However, Louise Mulford, a young scientist and an experienced diver, vomited suddenly, inhaled the vomit and choked. Despite frantic attempts to resuscitate Louise, she was pronounced dead at the Haslar Naval Hospital, 1 mile away. The whole diving team were stunned.

But if the risks of the project were great, the rewards were extraordinary.

As the work carried on, and to the astonishment to all concerned, slowly but surely a really large portion of the ship's hull was revealed, much larger than anyone could have ever dreamt. In the end, almost half of the hull was to be found intact, virtually the whole of one side, the starboard side. The ship was in a depth of 14 metres of water. The silts that had slowly completely buried her under the seabed were to also be her saviour. The ship and her contents were within a reduced oxygen environment, which ideally preserved them.

Over 19,000 objects were meticulously and carefully excavated, surveyed and lifted to the surface. Airlifts, which are a type of vacuum cleaner, were used to remove unwanted spoil down-tide (and the divers had to ensure they did not send any Tudor objects down-tide as well). Excavation revealed fragile and small objects such as wicker baskets, silk ribbons (both one ply and two ply), a velvet hat, bobbins, needles and thimbles. Among these objects were chests belonging to some of the 500 men who perished. Many contain their personal possessions. Through a study of these chests we have been able to identify their employment on the ship, such as the master carpenter and the barber surgeon.

Between 1979 and 1982, over 500 divers and diving archaeologists made a staggering 24,640 individual dives into the murky waters of the wreck. It was long and dark work. A total of nine man-years had been spent on the seabed. The divers were proving that archaeology could be successfully carried out underwater just as well as on land. A great achievement.

Extensive portions of three decks survived on the starboard side. The lowermost deck was the storage area for foodstuffs, longbows and arrows, rope lockers and spare rigging. The main deck was the principal gun-deck, with six guns found at gun-ports still on their carriages.

Interestingly in agreement with the ambassador's report just after the sinking, the gun-port lids were found open and the guns run out for action. The upper deck in the stern housed a cabin where some of the officers' chests were found, with the remains of the men who owned them. Divers worked from dawn to dusk. Following their dives, they wrote reports recording the positions of the artefacts they excavated. These 'dive logs' form the basis for placing objects back to where they originate from in relation to the ship.

Although a fighting vessel, she was also the workplace and living place for 200 mariners, 185 soldiers, thirty gunners and their officers. As the great timbers of the hull were uncovered, partitions and several intact cabins were revealed, their occupants and functions suggested by the objects found within. Skeletons of the men, together with their clothing, some still wearing the shoes they drowned in, and a lot of personal possessions, were found on all decks of the ship. In the hold and on the orlop (or the lowest) deck above, great barrels containing joints of beef were found. On the main deck, a gun in the process of being reloaded, on the upper deck handguns lay close to their ports, and loose longbows, sheaves of arrows and leather wrist-guards all confirm that the *Mary Rose* was well prepared for fighting in her final moments.

Detailed surveys of the structure were vital for planning how to lift the ship and how to support it during and after the lift.

Nineteen eight-one was a glorious year as the hull had been exposed and surveyed. It was possible to swim down the whole length of the three decks. Six guns on their carriages still remained in position on the main deck. Chests belonging to the master gunner and other officers had slid across the deck and come to rest against the outer wall of the cabin. Archaeologists perfected lifting the chests complete with contents to excavate on board *Sleipner*. By the time the diving season had ended in December 1981, all the guns had been lifted. Only a few areas such as the brick oven with built-in cauldron remained, each brick tagged, recorded and carefully prised from its mortar bed. Eventually, these were also lifted to surface.

It was necessary for deck-planks to be removed in preparation for the lift. They were placed in large containers next to the site ready for lifting. In total, over 800 internal timbers and the rudder and gun-port lids were removed prior to the lift. Corroded piles of shot and other iron concretions were loosened using pneumatic drills or, occasionally, with small explosive charges.

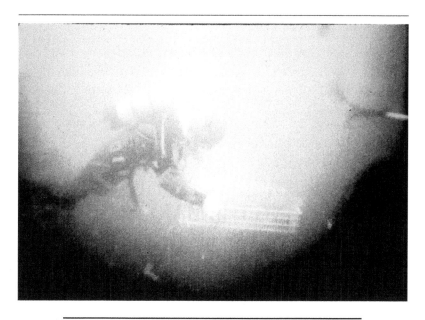

Figure 9 - A diver carries a tray with some smaller finds from the wreck site. Photo copyright © Philip Roberts

Figure 10 - Mary Rose Trust's diving vessel 'Sleipner' Photo copyright © Philip Roberts

RAISING THE MARY ROSE

The raising of the *Mary Rose* was a national event, the culmination of an extraordinary feat of engineering and technology.

The method to lift the ship required 170 wires to be securely attached to bolts through the hull of the ship and to a frame positioned over the ship and supported on four legs fitted with hydraulic jacks. While the *Mary Rose* divers drilled, tunnelled and fitted the lifting wires to the ship, a team of Royal Engineer divers prepared the seabed beside it for a lifting frame and cradle. By September 1982, *Tog Mor* was anchored astern of *Sleipner*.

At 9.03am on 11 October 1982, inch-by-inch, *Tog Mor* gently raised the *Mary Rose*, previously secured on her lifting cradle, out of the Solent. No one watching that day will ever forget the heart-stopping moment when a pin attaching the lifting frame to one of the legs gave way and there was a sudden jolt to the whole structure. Thankfully, there was no damage to the ship and the lift was a complete success. Alexander McKee described it as the most wonderful day of his life.

The *Mary Rose* surfaced to the sounds of klaxons blasting from the fleet of small vessels gathered to watch. From Southsea Castle, where Henry had witnessed the sinking 437 years earlier, a gun salute could be heard. Over 60 million people around the world watched the longest television outside broadcast yet undertaken, as the *Mary Rose*, between the lifting frame and cradle, was carefully lowered on to a barge for the short tow home to Portsmouth. Still lying on her side exactly as she had lain on the seabed, the *Mary Rose* was taken to the listed historic Dry Dock No. 3 in Portsmouth Historic Dockyard, only a few hundred metres from where she was built in 1510. On 11 July 1985, the ship was turned upright.

Figure 11 - The *Mary Rose* is lifted from the sea.
Photo copyright © Philip Roberts

Figure 12 - The *Mary Rose* is brought to land.
Photo copyright © Philip Roberts

Figure 13 - Conservation begins.
Photo copyright © Philip Roberts

THE CONSERVATION OF THE SHIP

A survey of wood samples was taken of the timbers to access their condition and to plan the conservation programme. Many of the 800 timbers removed from the wreck underwater were reinstated. Indeed, on 30 July 1990, the last orlop (lowest) deck planks were replaced. To stop the hull from drying out and rotting away she was sprayed with chilled water, a treatment which lasted for twelve years.

The reinstatement, in December 1993, of the very last timber in the initial restoration programme, marked the end of yet another phase in the history of the *Mary Rose*, and allowed the project to progress to active conservation.

The chemical chosen to replace much of the water, to stabilise her timbers and to strengthen the internal cellular structure, and increase the molecular weight of the timbers, was polyethylene glycol in solution, sprayed over the ship for almost twenty years. A new spray system was built to cope with the treatment programme. Completed in July 1994, this included over 500 metres of pipework and 320 stainless steel nozzles

Finally, at 7.27am on 29 April 2013, the sprays were turned off. Then she underwent air-drying to lock those wax chemicals into the wood, which was initially expected to take five years. This process was also a success. The intensive phase of air-drying was completed on 30 November 2015, allowing the final stage in the new museum building to take place.

HOW DO WE KNOW THAT THIS IS THE MARY ROSE?

None of the 19,000 objects found have the words 'Mary Rose' on them. But there is plenty of evidence, including inscriptions, coins, timber analysis, similarity of knives and shoes with known Tudor examples and historical records, this makes it obvious it is the *Mary Rose*. Notably, a large contemporary picture, the Cowdray engraving, shows the *Mary Rose* sinking in the same place in which she was found.

Evidence from dendrochronology shows that all the timbers on the ship are from trees cut down between 1443 and 1540. The objects in the ship are all from the right period. For example, inscriptions on the guns show that they were all made before 1544. Analysis of some of the gold coins shows that they were mixed with silver. This debasement of currency happened in 1545. The three half-sovereigns from the purser's chest were not minted until April 1545. And plates were found that belonged to Lord Lisle, the Admiral of the fleet in 1545, together with a large portion of a pewter dinner service with the initials GC, showing that they belonged to the captain, Sir George Carew, who we know went down with his ship.

Figure 14 - A parrel from the *Mary Rose.*
A parrel allows the mast to slide up and down to
either release or stow the sails.
Photo copyright © Philip Roberts

SAILING AND NAVIGATIONAL EQUIPMENT

Although most of the rigging was salvaged by the Tudors, parts of the standing rigging were discovered underneath the starboard side, some still attached to the ship. Cable lay on the upper deck amidships beside an iron anchor. On the storage deck was found a rigging store, with blocks, a spare set of parrels – trucks (balls) and ribs used to 'roll' the sail carrying yards up the mast – and a complete crow's nest or ship's top.

This was an age of exploration. Eleven years after the *Mary Rose* first sailed, Magellan circumnavigated the world. But the *Mary Rose* did not. Navigation and pilotage was crucial as many hazardous rocks lay close to the shore. In 1514, Henry established Trinity House to train mariners and maintain buoys and lights. The instruments found on the *Mary Rose* represent the toolkit of the navigator: compasses, tide calculator, sounding lead, log reel and sandglass. No charts survive, but chart sticks, dividers and a protractor did. It had always been assumed that the practice of mounting compasses on gimbals, so that the instrument would remain level despite the movement of the ship, had first been introduced no earlier than the seventeenth century. Yet there were three examples discovered on the *Mary Rose* from 1545. These are the earliest dated set of navigational tools in Europe.

Part of a ship's log was also discovered, a device that would have been at home on HMS *Victory* two centuries later. On the *Mary Rose* it would have been the very latest thing. The log was a device used for measuring the ship's speed. Details such as speed are still entered in the ship's log today, and the name 'logbook' has come into general use for recording data. It is amazing to discover how little some items have changed over the centuries. For example, the bosun's whistle found on the *Mary Rose* is almost identical to the bosun's whistle used on ships fighting in the Napoleonic wars.

WEAPONS OF WAR

The *Mary Rose* was a state-of-the-art warship. On her first voyage after being fitted-out, she carried seventy-eight guns. When she sank, she had ninety-one, excluding hand-held guns. Thirty-nine of these were large guns on carriages posted at ports cut into the side of the hull. The size of Henry's fleet was a statement of power and the actual clout came from the expensive bronze guns, many engraved with the royal emblem, the year it was made and the initials 'H' 'I' – 'Henricus Invictissimus' – meaning 'Henry most invincible'. Warfare at sea changed during the life of the ship, from being able to see your enemy face-to-face, to engaging the enemy at ever-increasing distances.

She carried a mixture of guns of different types and sizes for specific purposes and firing particular types of shot. On the main deck the most powerful modern long-range cast bronze guns stood beside wrought-iron guns with removable powder chambers. The wrought-iron guns were quick to load with stone shot, creating effective gashes in ships' sides at closer range. One such bronze cannon found in situ on the castle deck in the stern was a muzzle-loading bastard culverin made by Robert and John Owen in 1537. The term 'bastard' was used to describe any gun that did not conform to the standard proportions of its calibre. This one was both shorter in length and smaller in bore than a culverin of this period.

Here is a description of the sizes, weight and differences in style of some of the *Mary Rose* cannons and guns.

The demi-culverin was a medium bronze cannon similar to but slightly larger than the saker gun and smaller than a regular culverin. Barrels of demi-culverins were normally about 11 feet (3.4 m) long, had a calibre of 4 inches (10 cm) and could weigh up to 3,400 pounds (1,500 kg). It required 6 pounds (2.7 kg) of gunpowder to fire an 8-pound (3.6 kg) shot. The demi-culverin had an effective range of 1,800 feet (550 metres). The Fowler gun is a breech-loading gun. The main body of the cannon was formed of a tube opened at both ends. It has a separate powder chamber but the powder and ball was loaded together.

King Henry VIII supported home-grown weapon makers in London and Sussex. The first attempts to mass produce cast guns in iron are found in the hail-shot pieces recovered. Hand-held weapons included musket-type guns imported from northern Italy, the traditional yew longbow, anti-boarding weapons such as bills and pikes and, for close combat, the sword.

ARMAMENT

The mounted gun armament of the *Mary Rose* is listed several times and shows changes in her weaponry between 1514 and 1545. Here is a sample of some of the changes of weaponry in the listings:

	1514	1541	1545
Brass Guns			
Cannons	-	-	2
Demi-cannons	-	4	2
Culverins	-	2	2
Demi-culverins	-	2	6
Sakers	-	5	2
Iron Guns			
Demi-slings	2	-	3
Port Pieces	-	9	12
Fowlers	-	-	6
Bases (great and small)	-	60	30
Top Pieces	-	-	2
Hail Shot Pieces	-	-	20
TOTAL	78	96	91

CREW MEMBERS

THE CARPENTERS WHO KEPT THE MARY ROSE AFLOAT

The ship's carpenters were among the most important people on board the *Mary Rose*. Because the ship was wooden, they were very skilled professional workers. If something was needed to be repaired or made, then the carpenter was your man. They were on a par with the modern day naval engineers who maintain the ships of today. Their importance is evident in that they had a cabin of their own. Indeed, their cabin had even been extended during the ship's lifetime for their needs. It was on the main deck towards the stern.

Within the cabin and around the ship were found over 200 tools such as mallets, augers, planes, rulers, adzes, axes, hammers, handsaws, spokeshaves, gimlets, braces, chisels and whetstones. The tools are not that dissimilar to what we might find in someone's workshop today. Going by the quantity of different items, it is considered that there were up to six carpenters on board. On the deck just below the cabin, a single individual was found with his tools; a sawhorse, hammer, chisel, chopping block and tool holder. Was he fixing something here when the ship capsized? The chest belonging to the master carpenter contained some of the most expensive and beautiful possessions recovered. There were a total of seven chests found in the carpenter's cabin.

THE BARBER SURGEON WHO HELPED THE SICK

In the sixteenth century there was little understanding of disease. It was believed that illness was caused by an imbalance of the four humours (substances) that made up a person – blood, phlegm, black bile and yellow bile. Diagnosis by the colour, smell and taste of urine was common. Cures could be dietary, herbal or by the letting of blood. All these treatments were thought to bring the humours back into balance.

The crowded and busy living environment on the *Mary Rose* led to the potential for the spread of infection and sickness. Everyday duties on the ship brought its dangers, as evidenced by the thirty or more healed fractures observed on the crew's skeletons. While at battle, the risks of injury would have been even higher. Within a cramped unlit cabin on the main deck, the surgeon kept his tools. Apart from blood-letting, the surgery roles consisted of amputating wounded limbs and cauterising these to promote healing. Chisels, knives and saws were found for amputation purposes. The chisel would have been used to amputate small parts of the body such as fingers and toes, whereas hands, arms, feet and legs would have been operated on by the knife, to separate the flesh, and then the saw to cut through the bone.

The barber surgeon was also an apothecary, physician and dentist to the 500 men on board. Not all of the problems dealt with on the *Mary Rose* were caused by an accident or warfare. He could use his urethral syringe to inject mercury, to treat venereal diseases (particularly the French Pox, a venereal disease named after the enemy). The mercury would have temporarily eased the suffering but, unknown to the Tudors, would obviously do more harm than good in the long run. None of the human remains showed any signs of any sexual disease.

The merger of the Company of Barbers and the Fellowship of Surgeons to form the Company of Barbers and Surgeons in 1540 was appointed by King Henry VIII himself, as he was championing the English medical field to equal or better, that of other European countries. The barber surgeon was taught all medical trades and without obtaining a full university degree, not like doctors, who were certified and legal practitioners assisting the sick. So note that the barber surgeons were not called doctors. Similarly, today our surgeons, dentists and consultants in the UK and in some other countries, are not titled as doctor but simply as Mr, Mrs or Ms.

The distinctive surgeon's medical equipment found suggests that our surgeon was very experienced. He was, however, not a barber, despite belonging to the Company of Barbers and Surgeons. The company did not allow him to cut hair or shave another man's beard. Most of the best surgeons worked for the nobility. Our surgeon may have been employed by the captain, Vice-Admiral Sir George Carew.

The barber surgeon's cabin was 2.7 metres long and 2 metres wide. No furniture was found in there apart from a bench for preparing dressings, that is bandages soaked in herbal preparations. This suggests that the surgeon only worked here and that he slept and kept his belongings somewhere else. Indeed, a silk coif (a cap that covers the top, back and sides of the head) was found on the upper deck and this could be the one he wore for everyday use and on the day he drowned. Two wooden canisters were also found far away from his cabin, also on the upper deck close to the silk coif. Could he have been treating a sick crew member as the ship sank?

The only personal possessions found in the cabin was a velvet coif and a wooden chest that contained sixty-four objects. These included wooden lidded canisters containing ointments. One such canister contained peppercorns, a treatment for malarial fever, headaches, coughs and wind. Also in the chest were corked stoneware jars made in Germany, probably imported with their liquid contents, and rolls of pre-prepared dressings ready for use. A trepan for drilling into the skull, wooden ear cleaners and the handles of a number of other surgical tools were also found within the chest.

Glass bottles from the south of the Netherlands were found and poisonous materials such as mercury. Ceramic jars from Spain and Portugal were found still corked and held the remains of their medicines. One such jar, when it was first opened, still smelled of menthol. Ointments to soothe and heal were mixed and spread using spatulas also found in the chest. Only small amounts were needed to create a potion. The base for the surgeon's ointments was beeswax, butter or tallow. Into this he mixed resins, olive, poppy and fern oil, frankincense, sulphur, copper, lead and mercury.

The surgeon was a highly paid member of the crew and, although we do not know his name, his cabin, surgical chest and personal belongings reflect his importance.

THE SHIP'S PURSER

The ship's purser was just below the master in rank. His duties included paying and mustering the crew, keeping accounts of stores, buying supplies and issuing food and drink according to the ration list. He was also responsible for giving out clothing and for the safekeeping and distribution of lanterns and candles. There are pursers on warships even today.

The purser had a personal chest. In it he kept a pair of leather ankle boots, a knitted garment, a wooden comb and a knife. There was also a small square wooden plate, a leather drinking flask and his bowl marked on its base with the number 18. Also found were the tools of his job, his shives and spiles. A shive is a tapering wooden tap, which was hammered into a barrel so that the liquid inside could be poured out. A spile is a long bung that is tapped into the shive as a stopper to close the barrel. A wooden mallet found nearby would knock them into position.

The store was small and partitioned off from the rest of the deck. At one end was found a pile of seven gun-shields and at the other a number of lanterns. In the centre were chests full of clothes and tools. Among them were baskets, some with the remains of either fish or dried plums in them, and barrels, some of which held candles. Others still contained the residue of wine.

THE OFFICERS AND THE SAILORS

At sea, as on land, there was a huge social gap between officers and the men. The officers ate from elegant pewter tableware. They wore fashionable clothes trimmed with silk, the finest leather boots and the newest style in shoes. They had personal possessions neatly folded within sea chests containing purses with coins and dice for gambling. They had books, their own decorated pewter drinking flagons, wicker-bound wine flasks, pepper to add to their food and even some jewellery. By contrast, many of the men went barefoot on board, ate from wooden bowls, and wore simple clothing of leather, wool and linen.

From the remains of the surviving hull and the artefacts found within, it is now possible to build up a picture of life on board the *Mary Rose*.

The ship would have been quite crowded. Life on board would have been pretty grim. The ship would have been gloomy and fairly airless. The men never bathed or showered and facilities to have a wash were non-existent.

It is clear from the wreck that light only from port-holes or hatches would have caused a concern. Archaeologists discovered eight wooden lanterns found around the ship. Also found was a wooden candlestick with even a candle in it. It is these simple objects of wood, metal and leather, the mundane objects not heirlooms worth passing down the family line, that form the majority of the collection and teach us new things about everyday Tudor life. Indeed, we are still constantly learning about the Tudors from the *Mary Rose* and her objects.

Within the dark cramped hull the crew worked and played. On top of a barrel is a gaming board of Nine Men's Morris and there is a backgammon set.

The sinking of the *Mary Rose* has provided us with a unique insight into everyday objects, like looking into a Pieter Bruegel the Elder's painting.

COOKING FOR THE MEN

Deep in the hold is the 'kychen'. Two huge brass cauldrons, each holding up to 400 litres of liquid, were put within a brick housing, which included two wood-fuelled ovens accessed by arched entrances beneath the cauldrons. Each made with over 2,000 bricks and located either side of the keelson, the central internal backbone of the ship, this was the galley.

Bread would have been baked in the ovens, meat dangled over the oven entrance to roast, pottery vessels filled with separate meals for the officers, and muslin sacks would have been filled with peas or greens, floated within the cauldrons of simmering pottage. This was literally the Aga of its day.

Even ash was retrieved from below the cauldron. There was not much unburnt wood in the oven, so the fire was probably not lit when the ship sank. Over 700 logs were found. They were all about the same length (90cm), a practical size for loading, stacking and throwing into the oven. Some still have the bark on them.

It was also the domain of one of the most important men on board, the cook, paid as much as the master carpenter and the master gunner. One wooden bowl and a lid of a tankard had graffiti with the words 'NYE COEP COOK'. These two pieces of evidence suggest that Nye Coep was the name of the cook on the *Mary Rose*. A few possessions were found in the galley, such as a ladle and shoes that were probably the cook's. Like many of the crew, the cook carried a dagger. He also had a comb, his own wooden eating spoon and a few silver groats (a small amount of money).

A stool was found next to the ovens, making it the oldest dated type of this stool in the world. Another four-legged stool makes a good seat, but the cut marks on it show that the cook also used it as a chopping block.

The *Mary Rose* was probably carrying supplies for two weeks when she sank. This was a substantial amount. Evidence of the food on board was found within some of the thousands of silt samples taken during excavation. Some were obvious: the remains of 900kg half pig carcasses found near the galley; the eight barrels filled with 1,800kg portions of butchered cattle; barrels and baskets full of 750 cod or hake (cod almost a metre long, came from the fishing nets off Iceland and Newfoundland while hake probably came from English waters). All had been de-headed and gutted. There were conger eels, which had been caught from the Channel Islands, and a basket with plum stones. Also, contemporary documents list 3,150kg of hard, unsweetened biscuits and 31,500 litres of beer.

In 1545, there were 140,000 men in the English forces on land and at sea. This was almost twice the population of London at the time. Supplying food and drink to the fleet was the biggest problem in managing the king's ships. It was vital to keep the crew well-fed, so they were fit and ready to fight as well as to keep up morale. But, unlike the land army, which could forage for extra supplies, once the fleet was at sea it depended on what it carried. Methods of preserving food were usually limited to drying or salting.

Figure 15 - A recreation of a brick oven in the *Mary Rose*.
Photo copyright © Philip Roberts

Figure 16 - A small wicker bottle after preservation.
Photo copyright © Philip Roberts

Figure 17 - Peppermill with peppercorns and wooden domestic item. Photo copyright © Philip Roberts

Figure 18 - Barber Surgeon's ointment containers. Photo copyright © Philip Roberts

Figure 19 - A perfectly preserved wooden chest.
Photo copyright © Philip Roberts

Figure 20 - Selection of Gun Furniture.
Photo copyright © Philip Roberts

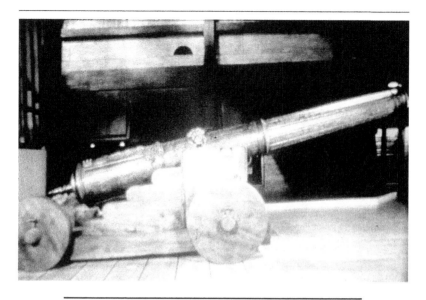

Figure 21 - A bronze muzzle loading bastard culverin cannon.
Photo copyright © Philip Roberts

Figure 22 - Backgammon board, book cover, nit comb and gold
coins. Photo copyright © Philip Roberts

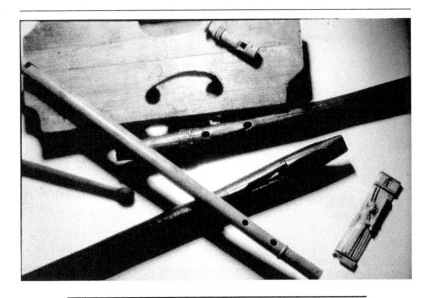

Figure 23 - Some musical instruments found on board.
Photo copyright © Philip Roberts

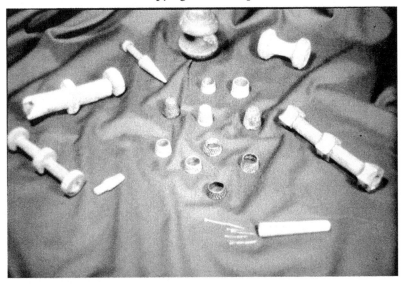

Figure 24 - Needlecraft Equipment.
Photo copyright © Philip Roberts

Figure 25 - Carpentry Tools
Photo copyright © Philip Roberts

Figure 26 - Navigation equipment.
Photo copyright © Philip Roberts

Figure 27 - The ship's bell of the *Mary Rose*.
Photo copyright © Philip Roberts

SOME OBJECTS FOUND

Since 1982, the ship's remains and contents have been accurately recorded, preserved and eventually displayed by teams of specialist maritime archaeologists, conservators and curators.

There are items such as the weaponry: mighty cannon; 139 complete longbows; over 3,500 arrows that were ready to shoot. But there are also small finds, like some tiny dice ready to be thrown to play a game. These are among thousands of personal items found on board and they can tell us huge amounts about Tudor life.

Most of the men carried wooden combs to remove nits and fleas, not just to tidy their hair. The crowded conditions on board inevitably led to the spread of these parasites. Another personal item was the linstock (a stick with a slow burning taper used to fire the cannon by touching the powder in the touchhole). Some of the forty-four linstocks recovered from the *Mary Rose* have decorative carved ends, such as a dragon's head to symbolise breathing fire or a hostile clenched fist, while others were just plain pieces of wood.

And the careful sieving of all samples meant that even the smallest remains, such as the residue of grapes from a seemingly empty barrel, could be identified. After conservation, objects have to be displayed or stored in a closely monitored environment with stable temperature and humidity. This is a true example of a time capsule. These are objects that just do not exist anywhere else.

MUSICAL INSTRUMENTS

Of the seven musical instruments recovered from the *Mary Rose*, three are whistle-type instruments, designed to be played with one hand, while a rhythmic accompaniment is provided by a tabor (or drum), played with the other hand. The longest tabor pipe, with the name E:LEGROS branded on a scroll, is in excellent condition, whereas the second is severely damaged. They are both made from cherrywood. They are extremely punishing to play, because of their inordinate stretch. In contrast, the third tabor pipe, made from boxwood and found in an officer's chest, is very comfortable to play. It bears the makers mark '!!', which appears on many instruments in continental museums and which has been associated with members of the Bassano family of instrument makers, several of whom settled in England between 1538 and 1540.

A 391mm-long cherrywood stick was found inside the E:LEGROS pipe. This provides an excellent beater for a tabor. The shell of one tabor, made of oak, was found in what was apparently a leather case. Traces of paint were identified before conservation, which strongly suggest black and red stripes. The bodies of two fiddles were found, both of rectangular construction, with incurved shoulders at the top and the bottom, carved from a single block of maple and with soundboards made from pine. A very simple bow, or "fiddlestick", was discovered among the artefacts during conservation.

The most significant and, indeed, unique find among all the musical instruments is a still or quiet shawm. This instrument is typically very like the modern oboe, but the cylindrical shaped

Mary Rose shawm is acoustically more akin to the modern clarinet than the oboe, playing an octave lower than might be expected. It was in two separate sections. The upper part was made out of boxwood and the lower part is made from cherrywood. All the complicated brass keywork survives. This shawm, therefore, is a brass instrument, a late example of the medieval instrument called the doucaine or dulcina. There is not another example of a still shawm anywhere in the world from this time. Indeed, until it was found, experts thought this instrument was not invented until fifty years later.

THE·SOLENT·ON·THE

HERE LIES A
MEMBER OF
THE SHIP'S
COMPANY
OF THE
MARY ROSE

19TH·JULY·1545·AND·WAS·RECOVERED·ON·THE

THE·KING'S·SHIP·MARY·ROSE·WAS·LOST·IN

May they rest in Peace
19th
JULY
1984

11TH OCTOBER 1982

Figure 28 - The memorial slate to those who died.
Photo copyright © Philip Roberts

THE UNTIMELY END

An engraved slab of welsh slate marks the resting place of an unknown member of the ship's company. On 19 July 1984, an anniversary of the sinking, a requiem mass was held in Portsmouth Anglican Cathedral to remember and give thanks for the lives of the 500 men who perished over four centuries earlier. Through a miracle of preservation, their deaths have left a rich legacy for generations into the future.

The significance of the group of skeletons found is that they are from the only Tudor warship we have in the entire world and it allows us access to ordinary people, which is really exciting. Everyone on board the *Mary Rose* was male. There was the captain and other officers, mariners, gunners, soldiers, a pilot, a purser, a surgeon, carpenters and cooks, to name only a few professions. There were more than 500 men on board and, of these, no more than thirty-five survived. There have been extensive studies of the skeletal remains of at least 179 individuals, ninety-two have been partially reconstructed. All were male, most in their 20s, the youngest around 10 years old and the oldest over 40. The average height was 1.71 metres (5' 7") only slightly smaller than UK males today. Human remains were found on all decks, the swiftness with which the *Mary Rose* sank did not allow time for escape.

Some had suffered childhood illnesses, mainly from malnourishment. There are healed fractures and some battle injuries, but in general they were healthy. Some bones have provided clues about the life of the person. Reactions to the stresses from routine use of heavy war bows or lifting heavy guns are visible on some joints, enabling the experts to suggest a profession.

For example, one man's bones tells us that he was between 25 and 30 years old and 5' 7" tall. He had well-developed muscles but his spine had signs of stress and his right elbow was badly damaged. He had the only ivory wrist-guard recovered, so he was an archer, or perhaps a captain of archers. Another crew member was a young man who had suffered a 'bowing' fracture of his right femur as a child. It is twisted, bowed and flattened and there is matching damage on his right pelvis. There was an older man who had suffered spiral fractures in his lower right leg. These were the result of a fall. It is clear that the bones were not reset after the fracture. A teenager had rickets as a child. This softens the bones and has allowed both tibias to bow. Rickets is caused from a lack of Vitamin D. A leg bone of another shows scars from healed scurvy. This is caused by a lack of Vitamin C and results in bleeding. On a long-bone like this leg bone, extra spurs occur at the spots where the blood clots. The heads of the upper leg bones of another are flattened and his hip joints are broad and shallow. This was caused by restricted blood flow to this area in childhood. Standing upright would have been impossible and he would have walked awkwardly. Some skulls have head wounds that may be battle injuries. One looks like an arrow wound but it was healed by the time the man died.

The master gunner has been identified as being younger than 35 years old. He had lost a lot of teeth and parts of his jaw bone had worn away, showing that he suffered from painful abscesses.

One of the complete skeletons recovered is of an archer, and he was found in the hold. Both his shoulders have a condition called *os acromiale*, where the tip of bone, the acromion, on the shoulder-blade has not fused. It usually fuses at the age of 18, but regular strain (such as archery) can prevent this. We can also tell from his tooth enamel that he was either an Englishman or a Welshman. The Welsh were well-known for their fame as archers in late medieval and Tudor times.

The cook's skeleton is virtually complete. It shows us that he was a man in his 30s, about 5' 6" tall and with heavy, strong bones. Evidence from his ribs and backbone suggests he spent most of his working life bent over. This strengthens the theory that he was the cook. At some stage in his life he broke a rib and his left foot.

The purser (person in charge of money and stores), was a robust and muscular man with good teeth and had an old head wound that had healed. He was in his 30s and about 5' 7" tall. The top of his leg bones and his hip joints are flat, so he must have walked with a rolling gait and would not have been able to straighten his back. With this physique, he could not have been an active member of the crew, which again suggests that he was the purser.

To help visualise individuals, facial reconstructions have been undertaken based on a study of their skulls. Using techniques more often used in forensic reconstructions of crime victims, the faces of nine people have been re-created. Further DNA tests of the human remains are still in process, and these may reveal other evidences such as whether some of the crew were from a foreign land, or not.

Similar scientific approaches have been used to identify the breed, colour and hair type of "Hatch", a small dog found near the door of the carpenter's cabin and named by the divers who found him. Remains of three rats were found. Perhaps Hatch did a good job at keeping their population down, or perhaps they were good swimmers, unlike most sailors of the day.

Before the human skeletons were displayed within the museum, a committee was set up as to whether it was appropriate to do so. The committee ran for eighteen months and after extensive surveys with the public, there were only two objections. The decision was to go ahead with the display. After all, the museum is primarily a memorial to all those who lost their lives with the *Mary Rose*. The importance of the ship and its contents is clear to all. The point of the museum is in the story told. It has to be the human one, to bring home to visitors that the men who died in the tragedy were real people, each of whom had his own position in the life of the ship. It is to be a lasting legacy to all those men who had sailed and died on the *Mary Rose*.

TO DISPLAY FOR ALL TIME

It certainly has been a hard graft for everyone involved in the Mary Rose Trust in the past forty years. Over 10,000 volunteers and staff have carried on throughout by giving their time, energy and money. Even before the ship was found, the Mary Rose 1967 Committee was formed to protect it when it was found. Among the objectives were "to display for all time in Portsmouth the *Mary Rose*" and "to establish, equip and maintain a museum or museums in Portsmouth to house the *Mary Rose* and related or associated material". This positive thinking is the force behind the whole project and, with no doubt, contributes to its continued success. The Mary Rose Trust adopted those objectives and, on the slow journey, has fulfilled them.

It is important that she would be seen not simply as a historic vessel in her own right, but also in the context of a historic dockyard that has developed over the centuries and close to other iconic warships from a later age, HMS *Victory*, HMS *Warrior* and HMS *M.33*.

Between February and October 1983, a huge building was built over the ship with a viewing bridge. On 11 October 1983, exactly a year after being raised, the *Mary Rose* was open to the public and a museum housing some of the objects the following year. The Mary Rose Exhibition Centre, right at the Portsmouth Historic Dockyard entrance, only displayed a few objects and the Ship Hall was at the other end of the dockyard next to HMS *Victory*. The Mary Rose Trust always saw these buildings as temporary solutions. The ultimate dream was always to house the ship and her collection together, within one building, as they were found, as it should be.

In 2005, it was decided to build a new museum over and around the ship while her conservation continued. This was a big challenge. The space available had a number of restrictions as the dry dock housing the *Mary Rose* is itself a Grade 1 Scheduled Ancient Monument. The architects chosen were Wilkinson Eyre and Pringle Brandon. The impression of the building is that of an oyster shell, with the *Mary Rose* the pearl at its centre. The museum is on three levels, with long galleries running the length of the ship opposite the lower decks, main deck and upper deck. Walkways between the galleries and the ship present views in one direction into the starboard side of the ship and in the other direction into the galleries, where the hundreds of objects are positioned opposite where they were found. At both ends of the walkways are further galleries that explore and interpret the story of the *Mary Rose* and her collection. The personal and professional belongings of specific crew members have been selected to present their stories and to provide unrivalled insights into the lives of officers and men at work and also at leisure.

THE MUSEUM'S FUTURE

After the air-drying had finished, the wall separating visitors from the ship could finally be removed. The Mary Rose Museum's design and construction was created with this in mind.

On 20 July 2016, the museum re-opened for the public to see the ship and her contents in a completely new setting. It is the world's largest environmentally controlled showcase with a completely clear view of the ship and of all the deck levels to the whole length of the ship. It is the best view of the *Mary Rose* since she was a sailing Tudor warship on the seas, indeed a great engineering and technical achievement that has cost £5.4 million. But after all is said and done, the museum is the only one in the world where you can see a genuine Tudor ship and experience the sensation as if you are actually on board it.

Trip Advisor gave the *Mary Rose* 99% positive feedback. The 1% negative comment was that 'the museum was just full of old stuff'. The *Mary Rose* is not virtual reality or of pretend material – the museum shows the real thing.

On 18 September 2015, the museum welcomed its millionth visitor, having opened just two years previously. Another extraordinary achievement for the *Mary Rose* story.

But the story does not end here...

Figure 29 - The New *Mary Rose* Museum.
Photo copyright © Philip Roberts

RECENT EXCAVATION

The raising of the hull in 1982 left a large hole in the seabed exposing the Tudor seabed beneath the ship. Any erosion to the sides of the hole could endanger objects buried around the site, and so a programme of regular site monitoring was initiated in 1983. Two decades after the raising of the *Mary Rose*, a dive vessel was back off the coast of Portsmouth. The wreck site was under threat from the Royal Navy, who wanted to dredge deep navigation channels next to the wreck site for two new aircraft carriers. They had just three weeks to investigate the site. Although the Ministry of Defence later decided not to go ahead with the dredging, in 2003 they provided the funding for the trust to undertake a study of the remains on the seabed.

From the vessel *Terschelling*, remote sensing provided a plan of magnetic hotspots, buried anomalies and surface features. All were investigated. A remote operated crawling vehicle was used, with fitted cameras, location devices and an airlift attached to a sieve to dig trenches into the spoil heaps that had built up on either side of the hull between 1979 and 1982.

Four hundred more objects were recovered, including another gold coin to add to the twenty-nine already found, another sundial and a large volume of collapsed timbers from the bow castle. On 11 October 2005, twenty-three years to the day since the ship was lifted, the end of the ship's 10m-stem was found (the huge timber that rises up from the keel and defines the shape of the bow) and an anchor. Excavation also revealed a portion of the missing port side of the ship in the bow and was reburied for future dives.

Conservation work continues behind the scenes on the ship's items, such as partitions, cabins, the stem, an anchor and companionways. It is hoped that one day these will be placed back with the ship.

AN ONGOING OBLIGATION

The unique legacy that has come about from the excavation and raising has brought upon the trust a commitment. This was understood and preserved within the aims and objectives of the Mary Rose 1967 Committee and later the trust, "To find, record, excavate, bring ashore, publish, report on and display for all time in Portsmouth, the *Mary Rose*." The trust has been successful in reaching all of these objectives, but it has an ongoing responsibility to maintain them.

Part of the legacy has been the acquisition of skills and the invention of techniques required to excavate, conserve and display the collection. These are being shared through internships within the trust and through the staff advising on or leading other projects, serving on committees that determine the future of these disciplines, and teachings at all levels.

The trust still has an ongoing commitment to the protection of the site where the *Mary Rose* lay. The Mary Rose Trust still holds a lease to the seabed in which any unexcavated remains of the vessel lie. Under the 1973 Protection of Wrecks Act, which designates an exclusion zone around the site, the trust holds the licence to dive. Portions of the forecastle still remain to be found. At present the trust will continue to monitor the site, assured that there is still more of the *Mary Rose* legacy for archaeologists to explore in the future.

Also, although what has already been recovered and investigated has revealed a great deal of information about the ship and its crew, there are also a great many questions still waiting to be answered. Some of these queries may very well remain unsolved.

One of the most exciting prospects for further research is the work on the human remains. Advanced methods for the extraction of ancient DNA may eventually make it possible to tell us which crew members came from what area of the country or provide information on hair and eye colour. These techniques could even be used to give us a more accurate count of just how many people died in 1545 and advance our understanding about the crew. We just do not know what technology may provide us with in the future. Things that seem impossible today may be possible in the future.

Internationally, the Mary Rose Trust has provided advice in Egypt, China, Peru, Cambodia and elsewhere, because others want to know about the principles the trust have worked under, such as should wrecks be raised from the bottom of the sea and how do you do it?

The Mary Rose Museum has won multiple awards, including a special commendation at the European Museum of the Year Awards 2015 and two awards at the Museums & Heritage Awards for Excellence 2014 in the Permanent Exhibition and Restoration/ Conservation categories.

CONCLUSION

"The *Mary Rose* is one of the most important objects in English history. It is up there with the Doomsday book, the Magna Carta and Hampton Court. Indeed, I would go further. The *Mary Rose* is the English Pompeii or Herculaneum, preserved by water, not by fire. All Tudor life is there from musical instruments to nit combs. Sporting events and great performances come and go as things of the moment; the *Mary Rose* is or should be, here forever." – David Starkey

So powerful and meaningful words from a prominent historian who is a very keen supporter of the *Mary Rose*.

BIBLIOGRAPHY

CSP: Calendar of Letters and Papers, Foreign and Domestic of the reign of Henry VIII, Preserved in the Public Record Office and the British Museum HMSO

Letters from the Mary Rose C Knighton and D Loades 2002

Sealed by Time, The Loss and Recovery of the Mary Rose Peter Marsden

The Mary Rose, The Excavation and Raising of Henry VIII Flagship Margaret Rule

The Mary Rose Revealed Alexzandra Hildred

The Mary Rose Museum, The Story Continues Anthony Burton

Mary Rose, Haynes Owner's Workshop Manual Brian Lavery

The Warship Mary Rose – The Life & Times of King Henry VIII's Flagship David Childs

Mapping Portsmouth's Tudor Past Dominic Fontana

ACKNOWLEDGEMENTS

The Mary Rose Trust

Chief Executive of The Mary Rose Trust, Helen Bonser-Wilton

Christopher Dobbs, Head of Interpretation at The Mary Rose Trust

Alex Hildred, Curator of Ordinance Mary Rose Trust

Sue Collis, Mary Rose Information Group Co-ordinator at The Mary Rose Trust

Sally Tyrrell, The Mary Rose Trust

Staff at The Mary Rose Museum Shop

Thank you to my children, Joseph and Susanna, for their love and patience while my time was spent writing this book. To my parents, Merfyn and Irene, for their continued love, support and genuine interest in my love of the *Mary Rose*. Thank you so much to Christopher Dobbs at the Mary Rose Trust for giving his time in sharing his invaluable knowledge, for proofreading my work, finding and correcting my mistakes and for being zealous in the future success of my book. To my publisher, Tim Ridgway, his wife Claire, and all the authors at MadeGlobal Publishing for their very kind support. Lastly, a huge thank you to Rachel McNeil and her mum Jenny for your love and kindness in sharing memorable and happy days together at various Tudor sites. I love you all.

ILLUSTRATIONS

ABOUT PHILIP ROBERTS

Philip Roberts is the author of *Whitehall Palace in a nutshell* and *The Mary Rose in a Nutshell*. He has been an active member of the *Mary Rose* Information Group for over twenty years, spreading the message of the *Mary Rose* story to various groups across the east of England. He is also a long-time Tudor re-enactor at many places including the Mary Rose Museum.

YOUR ROUTE THROUGH THE MARY ROSE MUSEUM

'The Story Continues' signs in each gallery directs you along the visitor route shown here

1   RECEPTION AND ENTRANCE

2   THE KING'S SHIP

The *Mary Rose* had a successful career from her launch in 1511 until a fateful day in July 1545. She was paid for by Henry VIII and his mark is to be found on many objects, from rigging blocks to the large bronze guns.

3   19TH JULY 1545

The *Mary Rose* was lost during a battle with an invading French fleet, much larger than Spanish Armada 43 years later. There are many theories on why she sank but we will never be certain. But we do know that 500 men lost their lives.

4   THE MAIN DECKS

Thousands of objects have been recovered from the seabed. Opposite the remains of the hull many of these – the guns, their carriages and all the ship's equipment – are arranged as they would have been on the ship minutes before she sank.

5   MEN OF THE MAIN DECK

The cabins of the Master Carpenter and the ship's surgeon were on the main deck. The wreck contained a very large number of woodworking tools, medicine containers and pieces of medical equipment. Also found on this deck was a chest belonging to the Master Gunner, a key figure on this floating gun platform.

Go down the stairs to continue your visit. Alternatively, please use the nearby lift.

6   SCIENCE AND THE MARY ROSE

The *Mary Rose* and her objects have been saved through many scientific techniques. Research has revealed much about the ship and her crew.

7   THE LOWER DECKS

The ship's provisions and spare equipment were stored in the bottom levels of the ship. Here too was the ship's gallery, found under four metres of mud.

8   MEN OF THE LOWER DECKS

The ship's large collection of cooking utensils allows us to reconstruct much of how the crew and officers were fed. Other objects recovered from the lower decks tell us how the men spent their time, at work and at leisure.

9   MARY ROSE VIEWING LIFT

This lift rises from the bottom of the ship to the upper decks and gives spectacular views of the ship's hull. **If you do not wish to use the lift, please go up two flights of stairs to the Upper Decks.**

10   MEN OF THE UPPER DECKS

The ship's officers had their cabins on the upper and castle decks. It was also here that the soldiers stood, armed with longbows, swords, pikes or muskets to attack the enemy.

11   HANDS ON THE MARY ROSE

Test your strength and skill with weapons such as the longbow and pike.

Special demonstrations are held every week – see notices for timings.

12   THE UPPER DECKS

The upper deck was covered with a net to stop the enemy boarding the ship. Sadly, it also trapped a great many of the *Mary Rose's* crew making it impossible for them to escape the sinking ship.

13   THE ADMIRAL'S GALLERY

Unlike the crew, the officers had fine pewterware to eat and drink from, books to read and fashionable clothes to wear. Even some of the musical instruments they listened to have survived.

14   DIVERS' STORIES

The excavation and recovery of the *Mary Rose* was the largest underwater archeological project ever undertaken, a huge achievement involving hundreds of people, professional and amateur.

15   MUSEUM SHOP AND CAFÉ

Entrance & Exit

The Mary Rose

ISBN: 978-84-943721-1-7

In **Mary Boleyn in a Nutshell**, **Sarah Bryson** discusses the controversies surrounding Mary Boleyn's birth, her alleged relationships with two kings, her portraiture and appearance, and her life and death. Mary survived the brutal events of 1536 and was able to make her own choices, defying the social rules of her times by marrying for love. It is from Mary that the Boleyn bloodline extends to the present day.

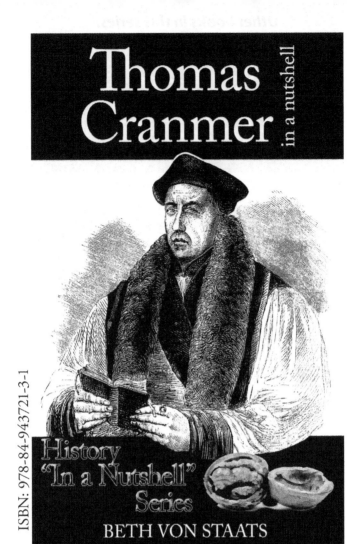

ISBN: 978-84-943721-3-1

Thomas Cranmer
in a nutshell

History
"In a Nutshell"
Series

BETH VON STAATS

In **Thomas Cranmer in a Nutshell**, **Beth von Staats** discusses the fascinating life of **Thomas Cranmer**, from his early education, through his appointment to Archbishop of Canterbury, his growth in confidence as a reformer, the writing of two versions of the English Book of Common Prayer and eventually to his imprisonment, recantations and execution.

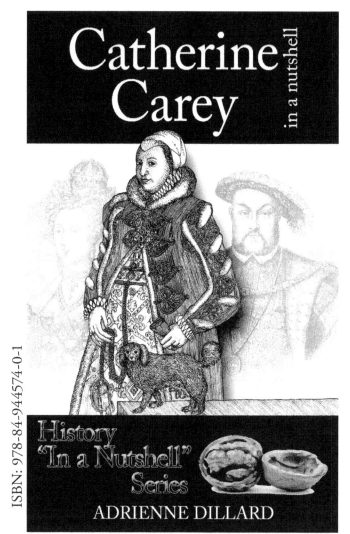

Catherine Carey
Carey

in a nutshell

ISBN: 978-84-944574-0-1

History
"In a Nutshell"
Series

ADRIENNE DILLARD

Catherine Carey in a Nutshell examines the life of Catherine Carey, daughter of Mary Boleyn, from the controversy surrounding her paternity through her service to Henry VIII's queens, the trials of life in Protestant exile during the Tudor era, and the triumphant return of the Knollys family to the glittering court of the Virgin Queen. This book brings together what is known about one of Queen Elizabeth I's most trusted and devoted ladies for the first time in one concise, easy-to-read book.

Sweating Sickness

in a nutshell

ISBN: 978-15-009962-2-2

History "In a Nutshell" Series

CLAIRE RIDGWAY

In **Sweating Sickness in a Nutshell**, Claire Ridgway examines what the historical sources say about the five epidemics of the mystery disease which hit England between 1485 and 1551, and considers the symptoms, who it affected, the treatments, theories regarding its cause and why it only affected English people.

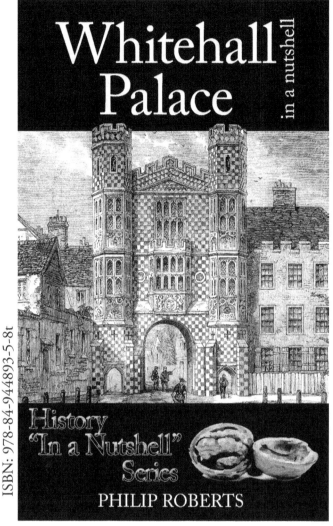

Whitehall Palace

in a nutshell

History
"In a Nutshell"
Series

PHILIP ROBERTS

ISBN: 978-84-944893-5-8t

In **Whitehall Palace in a Nutshell**, researcher and author *Philip Roberts* delves into the history of England's most important and significant lost building, a palace which had 2000 rooms and covered 23 acres in its heyday.

Using his unprecedented connections, Philip has been able to gain access to the historical places in Whitehall Palace which still exist today, many of which are not open to public access.

Philip Roberts, a member of the Mary Rose Trust Information Group Team for well over 20 years, has a passion for Tudor re-enactment and educating people about history.

Edward VI
in a nutshell

ISBN: 978-84-945937-0-3

History "In a Nutshell" Series

KYRA KRAMER

Born twenty-seven years into his father's reign, Henry's VIII's son, Edward VI, was the answer to a whole country's prayers. Precocious and well-loved, his life should have been idyllic and his own reign long and powerful. Unfortunately for him and for England, that was not to be the case. Crowned King of England at nine years old, Edward was thrust into a world of power players, some who were content to remain behind the throne, and some who would do anything to control it completely. Devoutly Protestant and in possession of an uncanny understanding of his realm, Edward's actions had lasting effects on the religious nature of the kingdom and would surely have triggered even more drastic changes if he hadn't tragically and unexpectedly died at the age of fifteen.

Henry VIII's Health
in a nutshell

History "In a Nutshell" Series

KYRA KRAMER

ISBN: 978-84-944574-2-5

Tudor histories are rife with "facts" about Henry VIII's life and health, but as a medical anthropologist, Kyra Kramer, author of Blood Will Tell, has learned one should never take those "facts" at face value. In Henry VIII's Health in a Nutshell, Kramer highlights the various health issues that Henry suffered throughout his life and proposes a few new theories for their causes, based on modern medical findings.

Known for her readability and excellent grasp of the intricacies of modern medical diagnostics, Kyra Kramer gives the reader a new understanding of Henry VIII's health difficulties, and provides new insights into their possible causes.

HISTORY IN A NUTSHELL SERIES

Sweating Sickness - **Claire Ridgway**   Catherine Carey - **Adrienne Dillard**
Mary Boleyn - **Sarah Bryson**   The Pyramids - **Charlotte Booth**
Thomas Cranmer - **Beth von Staats**   The Mary Rose - **Philip Roberts**
Henry VIII's Health - **Kyra Kramer**   Whitehall Palace - **Philip Roberts**

NON FICTION HISTORY

Anne Boleyn's Letter from the Tower - **Sandra Vasoli**
Jasper Tudor - **Debra Bayani**
Tudor Places of Great Britain - **Claire Ridgway**
Illustrated Kings and Queens of England - **Claire Ridgway**
A History of the English Monarchy - **Gareth Russell**
The Fall of Anne Boleyn - **Claire Ridgway**
George Boleyn: Tudor Poet, Courtier & Diplomat - **Ridgway & Cherry**
The Anne Boleyn Collection - **Claire Ridgway**
The Anne Boleyn Collection II - **Claire Ridgway**
Two Gentleman Poets at the Court of Henry VIII - **Edmond Bapst**
A Mountain Road - **Douglas Weddell Thompson**

HISTORICAL FICTION

The Devil's Chalice - **D.K.Wilson**
Falling Pomegranate Seeds - **Wendy J. Dunn**
Struck with the Dart of Love: Je Anne Boleyn 1 - **Sandra Vasoli**
Truth Endures: Je Anne Boleyn 2 - **Sandra Vasoli**
The Colour of Poison - **Toni Mount**
Between Two Kings: A Novel of Anne Boleyn - **Olivia Longueville**
Phoenix Rising - **Hunter S. Jones**
Cor Rotto - **Adrienne Dillard**
The Claimant - **Simon Anderson**
The Truth of the Line - **Melanie V. Taylor**

CHILDREN'S BOOKS

All about Richard III - **Amy Licence**
All about Henry VII - **Amy Licence**
All about Henry VIII - **Amy Licence**
Tudor Tales William at Hampton Court - **Alan Wybrow**

PLEASE LEAVE A REVIEW

If you enjoyed this book, *please* leave a review at the book
seller where you purchased it. There is no better way to thank
the author and it really does make a huge difference!
Thank you in advance.

Lightning Source UK Ltd.
Milton Keynes UK
UKOW05f1817020317
295761UK00023B/631/P